PIANO MEDITATIONS

12 original piano pieces inspired by contemplative works of art

PAM WEDGWOOD

FABER *ff* MUSIC

INTRODUCTION

I have always thought that when art and music are combined in a special way, they can bring new meaning into our lives. The pieces in this collection are all inspired by works of art on themes of mindfulness, meditation and reflection. I have tried to portray my own interpretation of the artworks with strong melody lines and changing moods, and I hope the art will stimulate and encourage you to interpret each piece in your own special way. Why not try to create your own music inspired by the artworks, too. Be at peace and enjoy!

Pam Wedgwood

© 2020 by Faber Music Ltd
This edition first published in 2020
Bloomsbury House
74–77 Great Russell Street
London WC1B 3DA
Music processed by Jackie Leigh
Cover design by Chloë Alexander
Cover image: *Meadow*, Sisley (Ailsa Mellon Bruce Collection)
Printed in England by Caligraving Ltd
All rights reserved

ISBN10: 0-571-54153-4
EAN13: 978-0-571-54153-9

To buy Faber Music publications or to find out about the full range of titles available
please contact your local music retailer or Faber Music sales enquiries:

Faber Music Ltd, Burnt Mill, Elizabeth Way, Harlow CM20 2HX
Tel: +44 (0) 1279 82 89 82   Fax: +44 (0) 1279 82 89 83
sales@fabermusic.com   fabermusicstore.com

CONTENTS

At Sunset   4

As Morning Awakes   6

The Journey   8

Rise Up   11

Reflections   14

Rocken End   16

Waiting   18

Changing Moods   20

Chant   23

Just a Perfect Day   26

Looking on the Bright Side   28

Danse espagnole   30

At Sunset
"Mortlake Terrace" (Turner)

Pam Wedgwood

There is something very romantic about a sunset, and Turner's painting is a perfect example.
The piece is written with this romantic feel in mind, the main melodic theme representing the long
shadows cast by the trees. Be sure to make the theme sing from the outset.

"There is nothing more musical than a sunset." — Claude Debussy

© 2020 Faber Music Ltd. All Rights Reserved.

As Morning Awakes 早晨醒來
"Chinese Landscape"

Pam Wedgwood

In this simple but atmospheric Chinese artwork I imagine dawn breaking over the mountain and the birds awakening.
The piece opens with a gentle pentatonic melody and gradually the music becomes more rhythmic.
At bar 7, imagine there is a soft drum beat in the background.

"Let every dawn be to you as the beginning of life, and every setting sun be to you as its close." — John Ruskin

© 2020 Faber Music Ltd. All Rights Reserved.

The Journey
"Abstract Landscape"

Pam Wedgwood

I imagine that each subject of this painting is on a journey; the birds are in flight and the boats are about to set sail. Each section of the piece represents a different stage of this journey. Play with conviction, observing all expressive markings, and be sure to make the melody sing at bar 13.

"Life seems to be a journey, each twist and turn producing a different ending." — Pam Wedgwood

© 2020 Faber Music Ltd. All Rights Reserved.

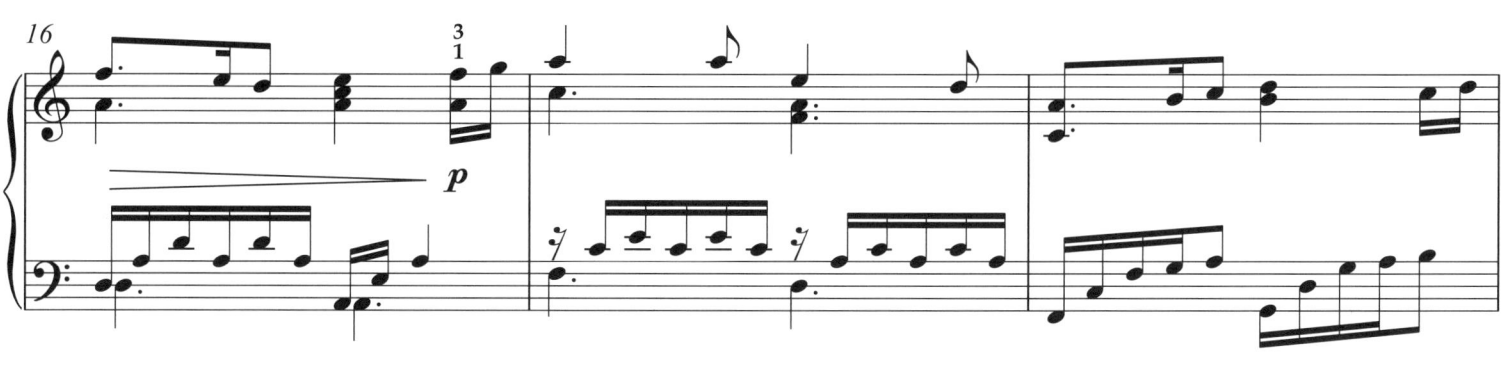
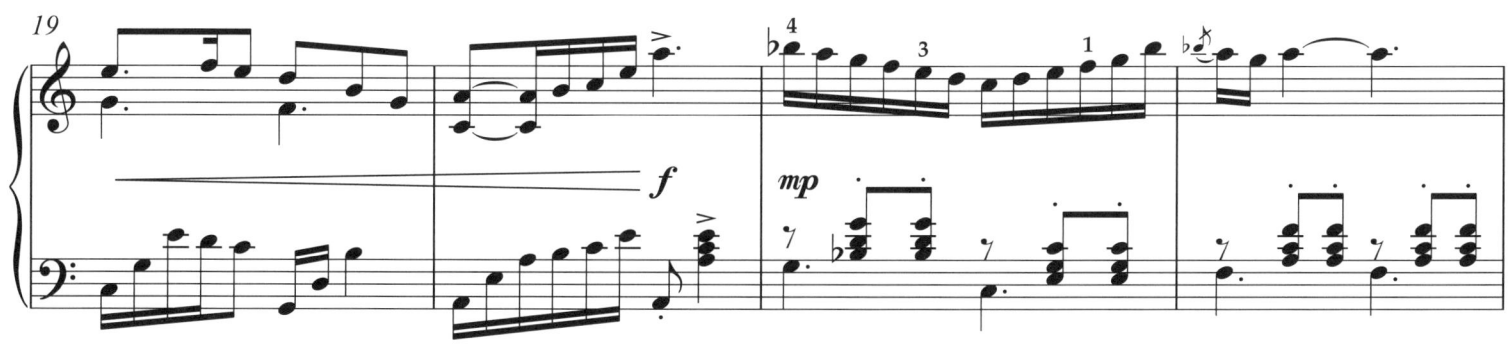
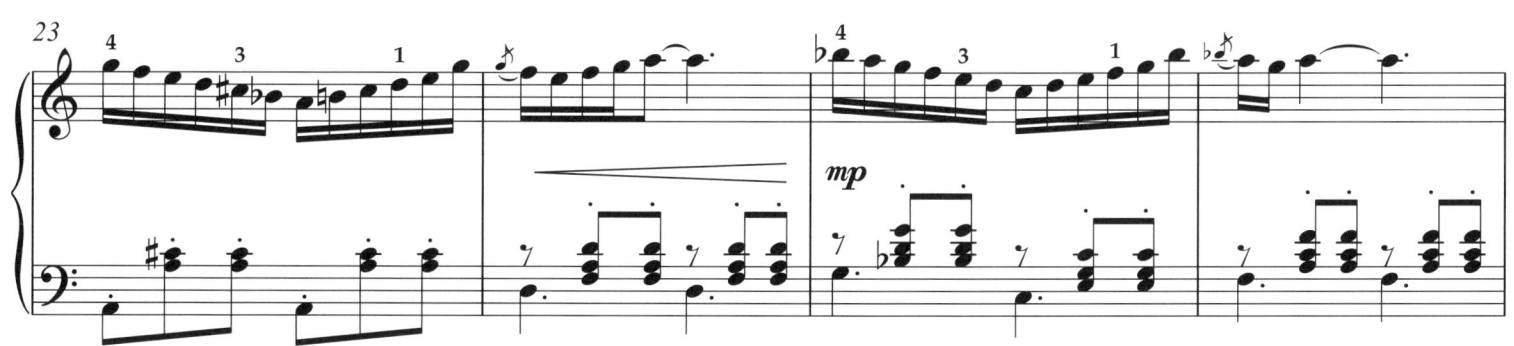

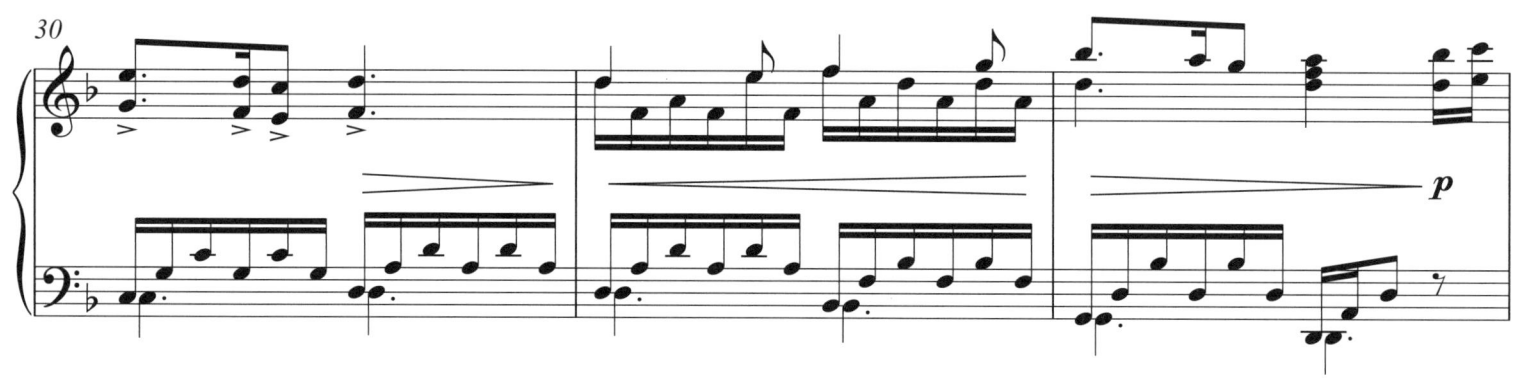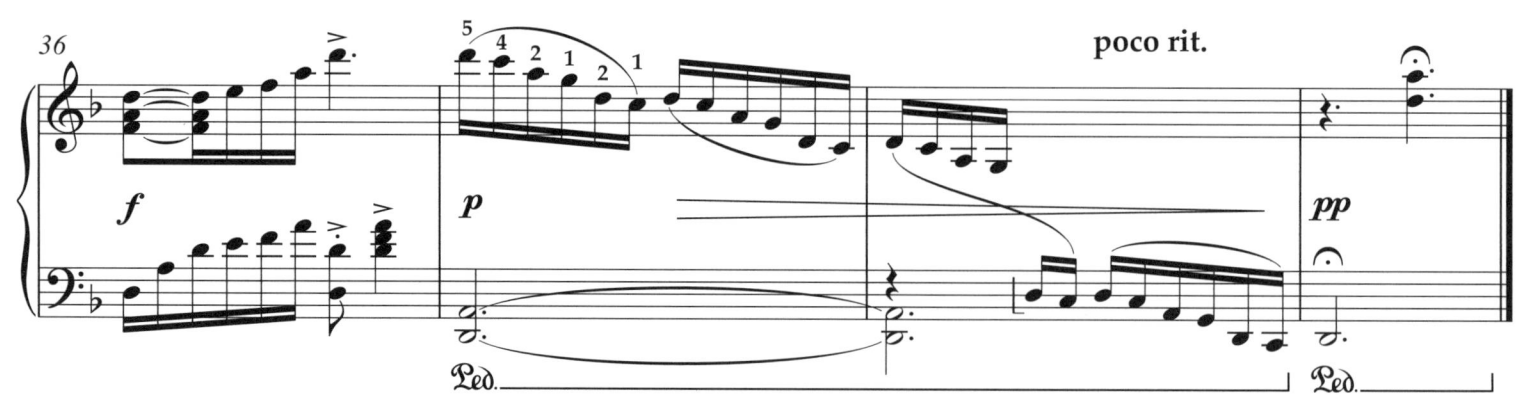

Rise Up
"Parliament in London" (Monet)

Pam Wedgwood

In this magical setting Monet depicts the sun gently breaking through the early morning mist. In my interpretation I introduce the chimes of Big Ben to set the scene, culminating in the sun rising as the piece comes to a dramatic close. Play peacefully and in a romantic style.

"In spite of everything I shall rise again: I will take up my pencil, which I have forsaken in my great discouragement, and I will go on with my drawing." — Vincent Van Gogh

© 2020 Faber Music Ltd. All Rights Reserved.

Reflections
"Solitude" (Pike)

Pam Wedgwood

I have written this piece in a light and airy style with jazzy rhythms and phrases. As you play, you will discover quite a few changes of direction! Try to imagine what each section suggests to you and play with style and freedom.

"The best thinking has been done in solitude." — Thomas Edison

© 2020 Faber Music Ltd. All Rights Reserved.

Rocken End

"Rocken End" (Beale)

Pam Wedgwood

Rocken End is one of my favourite beaches here on the Isle of Wight. As you play the opening bars, imagine the sea gently lapping over the golden sands. Then enjoy the boldness of the music at bar 25.

"My soul is full of longing / for the secret of the sea, / and the heart of the great ocean sends a thrilling pulse through me." — Henry Wadsworth Longfellow

© 2020 Faber Music Ltd. All Rights Reserved.

Waiting
"Boats at Low Tide" (Knights)

Pam Wedgwood

Charles Knights' watercolour scene of Bermuda captures boats waiting expectantly at low tide.
Play the opening bars dramatically, building towards the climax in bar 8. The melodic runs represent the
water slowly rising, then eventually subsiding for a calm ending – all is well!

"Time and tide wait for no man." — Geoffrey Chaucer

© 2020 Faber Music Ltd. All Rights Reserved.

Changing Moods: 1. Feeling Calm

"Sky Blue" (Kandinsky)

Pam Wedgwood

The brightly coloured floating shapes in Kandinsky's painting suggest an escape from reality.
This piece is in three movements, each with a different mood to explore.
Transport yourself to a dream-like place!

"How to be happy: decide every morning that you are in a good mood!" — Anon.

© 2020 Faber Music Ltd. All Rights Reserved.

2. Feeling Kind of Groovy

Pam Wedgwood

Let yourself go in this movement, relax and enjoy.

3. Feeling Blessed

Pam Wedgwood

Think about all the good things in your life when you play this final movement.

Chant
"Ascension"

Pam Wedgwood

I imagined being in an abbey or monastery listening to the sounds of ancient chant when I composed this piece. The reflections in the water, together with the warmth of the sun and the central spire surrounded by people make for an idyllic setting. Imagine yourself in a place of peace as you play.

"In a world of peace and love, music would be the universal language." — Henry David Thoreau

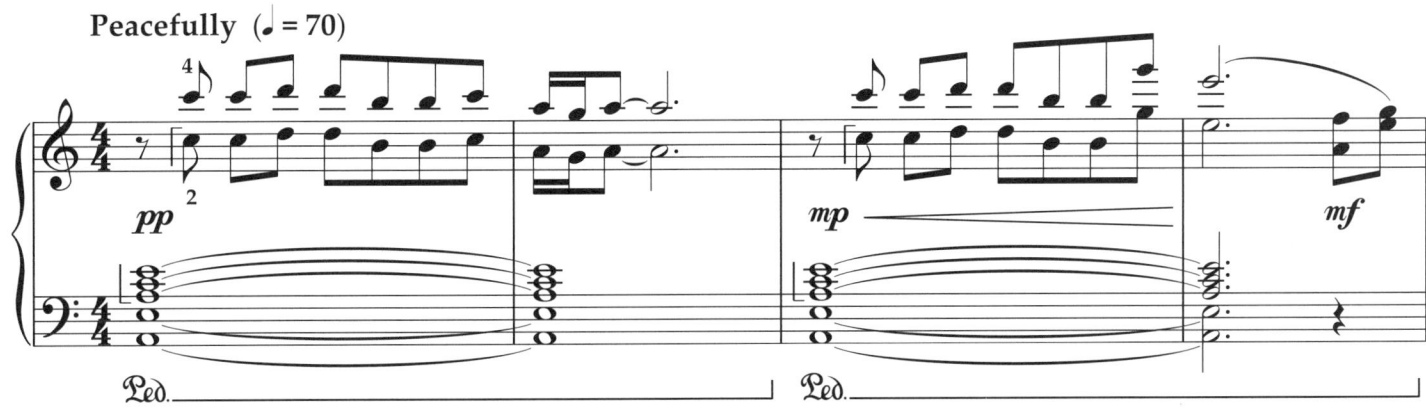
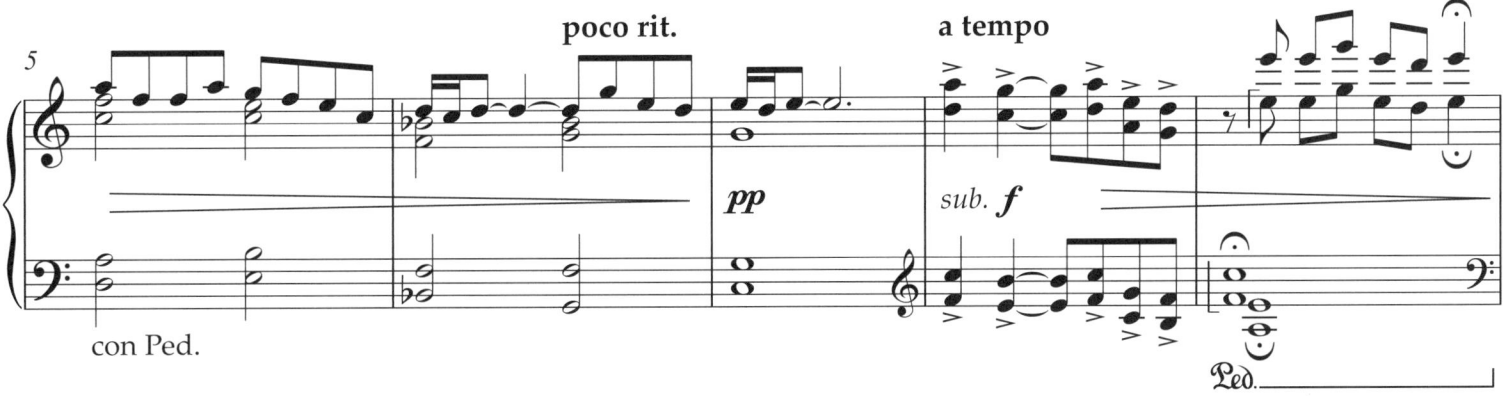

© 2020 Faber Music Ltd. All Rights Reserved.

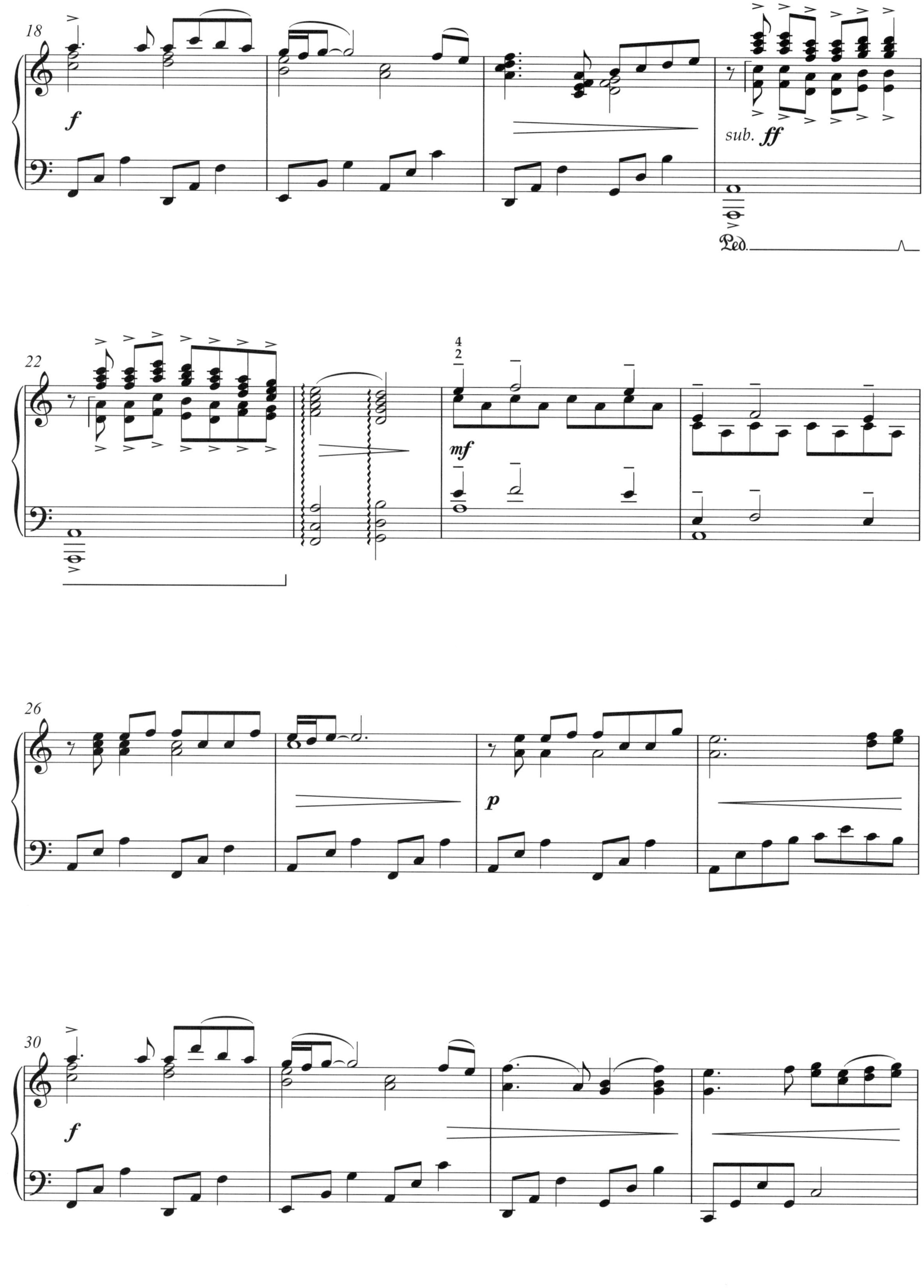
18
f
sub. ff
Ped.
22
4
2
mf
26
p
30
f

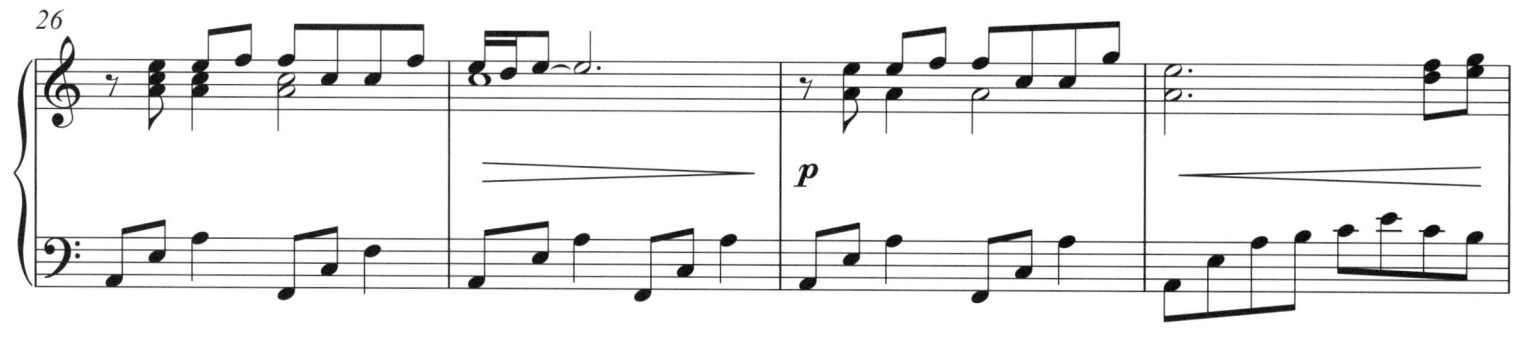

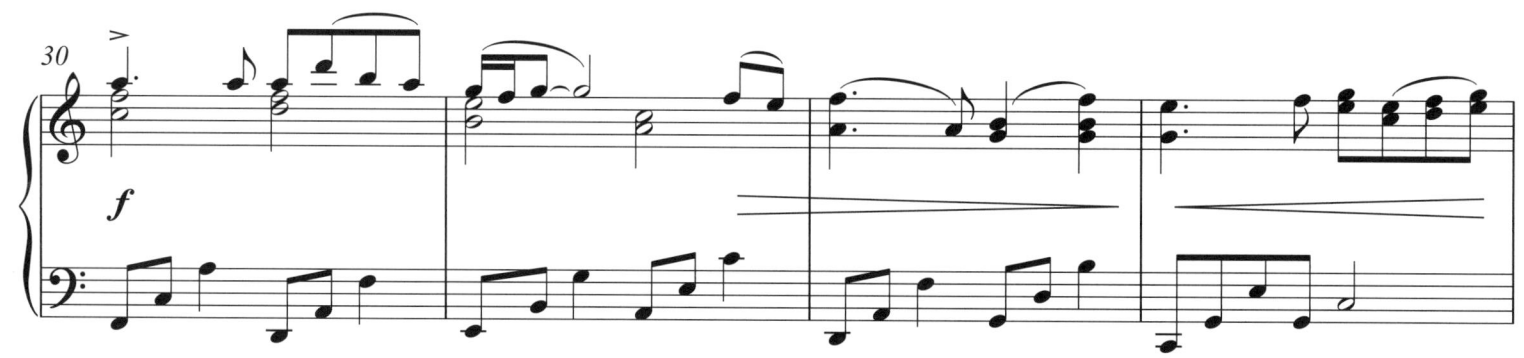

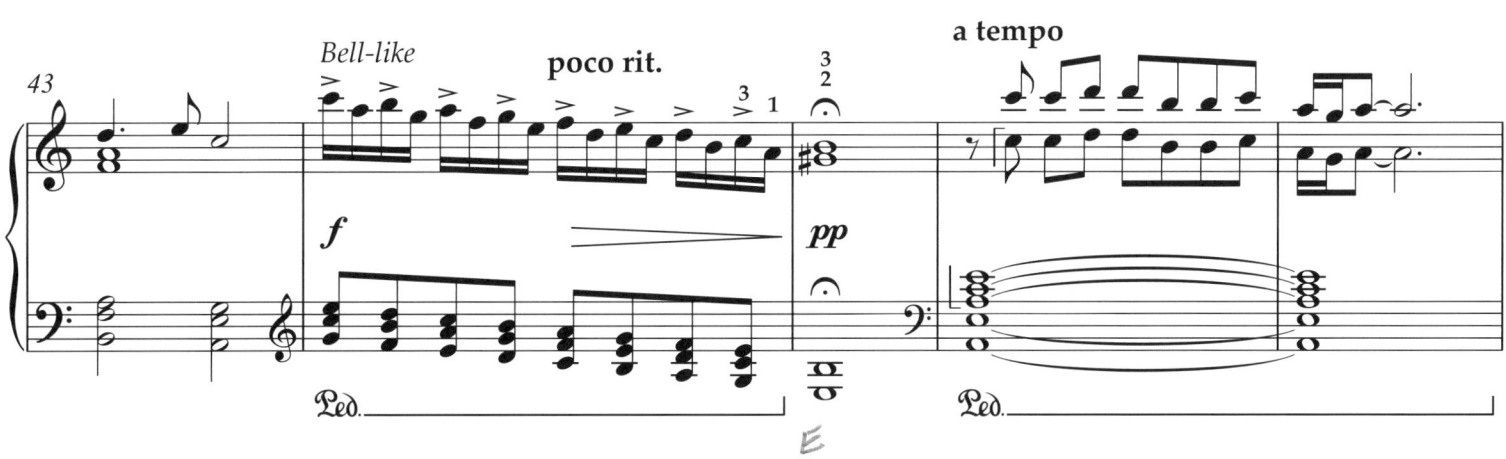
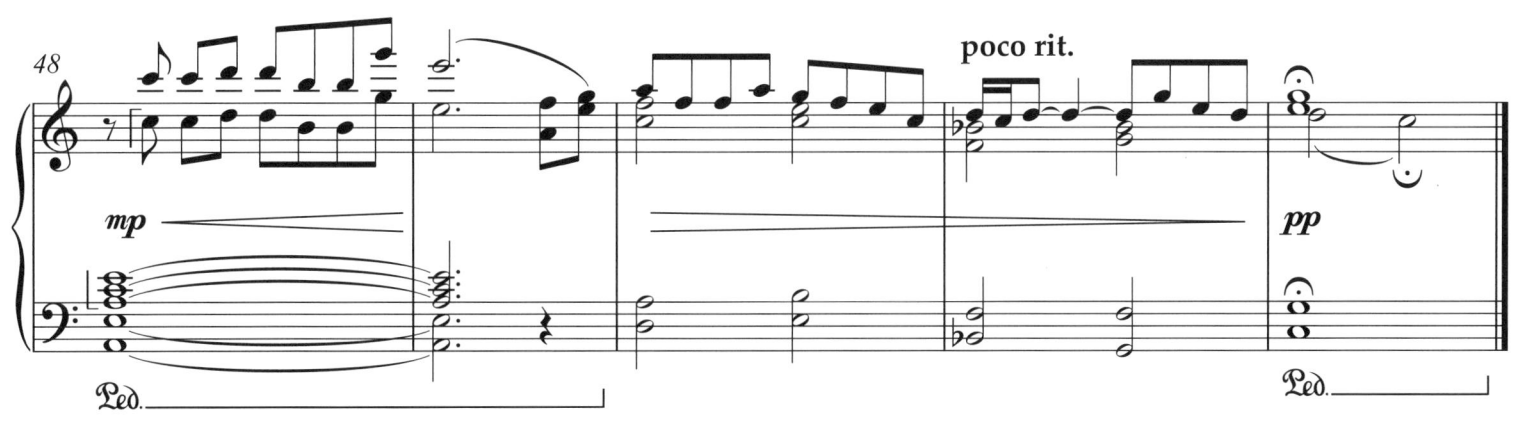

Just a Perfect Day

"Meadow" (Sisley)

Pam Wedgwood

Sisley's painting to me sums up a perfect summer's day; from the wild flowers in the foreground to the girls with their blue dresses and straw hats. Play the opening jazz waltz rhythm with a carefree swing!
Be sure to observe the change from swing to straight tempo at bar 28.

"Give every day the chance to become the most beautiful day of your life." — Mark Twain

© 2020 Faber Music Ltd. All Rights Reserved.

Looking on the Bright Side
"Abstracts, The Art"

Pam Wedgwood

This contemporary artwork to me depicts a setting sun but everyone is sure to have a different interpretation. What do you see in this painting? Play the piece with an element of fun and an air of optimism!

"Always Look on the Bright Side of Life" — Monty Python

© 2020 Faber Music Ltd. All Rights Reserved.

Danse espagnole
"Spanish Dancer" (Toulouse-Lautrec)

Pam Wedgwood

The sound of a Latin rhythm always makes me want to get up and dance! Abandon your
inhibitions in this piece and allow yourself to be transported to a Spanish fiesta.
Play at a speed you can manage, with lots of energy.

"And hand in hand, on the edge of the sand, / They danced by the light of the moon." — Edward Lear

© 2020 Faber Music Ltd. All Rights Reserved.

AFTER HOURS

Alarm clocks, barking dogs, telephones, meetings and rush hour … the hustle and bustle of life. What better way to relax than to sit down at the piano, chill out and indulge yourself with music from Pam Wedgwood's *After Hours*?

With a variety of pieces in styles to suit any mood—sentimental ballads to cosy dinner jazz, wistful blues to cheerful, upbeat tunes—***After Hours*** provides the perfect antidote to stress. So conjure up the dimly lit atmosphere of a jazz club, and relax with these lush harmonies and laid-back melodies …

Book 1 *grades 3–5* ISBN 0-571-52110-X	**Jazz Book 1** *grades 3–5* ISBN 0-571-52908-9	
Book 2 *grades 4–6* ISBN 0-571-52111-8	**Jazz Book 2** *grades 4–6* ISBN 0-571-52909-7	
Book 3 *grades 5–6* ISBN 0-571-52259-9	**Jazz Book 3** *grades 4–6* ISBN 0-571-53631-X	
Book 4 *grades 6–8* ISBN 0-571-53336-1	**Christmas** *grades 4–6* ISBN 0-571-52362-5	
Piano Duets *grades 4–6* ISBN 0-571-52260-2	**Christmas Jazz** *grades 4–6* ISBN 0-571-53337-X	

To buy Faber Music publications or to find out about the full range of titles available please contact your local music retailer or Faber Music sales enquiries:

Faber Music Ltd, Burnt Mill, Elizabeth Way, Harlow CM20 2HX
Tel: +44 (0) 1279 82 89 82   Fax: +44 (0) 1279 82 89 83
sales@fabermusic.com   fabermusicstore.com